STREET GRAPHICS
TOKYO

with 151 colour illustrations

Thames & Hudson

For my son, Joe

THANKS TO
Tokyo: Kaori Igarashi, John Sanders and Richard Stein
Oxford: Andre DeFries

A special thank you to all creators and collectors
of street graphics in Tokyo, especially:
Asako Toyoizumi for her beautiful *shodo* motifs,
which give each chapter title in traditional Japanese
Kanji calligraphy.
Andrew Watt, whose assistance in Tokyo and
contribution to the book are evident between fly
and endpapers.
The young Tokyoites of Harajuku for sharing their
street theatre and kindly indulging my photography
over the Sundays of June and October 2001.

SOURCES
Donald Richie, *Tokyo: a View of the City*, Reaktion,
London, 1999
Andrew Watt (ed.), *The Truth about Japan*, Yenbooks,
Tokyo, 1988
Yamamoto Tsunetomo, *Hagakure: the Book of
the Samurai*, Kodansha, Tokyo, 1979
Tokyo Q, Stone Bridge Press, Berkeley, 2001
Urban C. Lehner (ed.), *Let's Talk Turkey (about
Japanese Turkeys) and other tales from the Asian
Wall Street Journal*, Tuttle, Boston, 1996
Blade Runner, dir. Ridley Scott, 1982

First published in the United Kingdom in 2002 by
Thames & Hudson Ltd, 181A High Holborn, London WC1V 7QX

www.thamesandhudson.com

British Library Cataloguing-in-Publication Data
A catalogue record for this book is available from
the British Library

ISBN 0-500-28379-6

Printed in Hong Kong by H & Y Printing Limited

STREET
GRAPHICS
TOKYO

CONTENTS

La Flamme d'Or, by French designer and architect Philippe Starck, is referred to locally as 'The Golden Turd'. It lies on a polished granite plinth outside Starck's Super Dry Hall, the Tokyo HQ of the Asahi Brewery Corporation.

INTRODUCTION

'THERE IS NO JAPAN LIKE TOKYO.'

Lafcadio Hearn, 1895

The only Asian city in the world's 'Big Five' created a large canvas for its street imagery through unparalleled urban development. Tokyo has become a surreal cityscape, a theme park created by design, established through juxtaposition – its closest imitator, Disneyland. A corporate skyline of 'trophy architecture', borrowed landmarks and giant sculptures invites comparisons with an overturned toy box. The city has not one but twenty-three centres or *Kus* – each one teems with signs, symbols and images, from traditional handicrafts to huge computerized displays. Traditional Japan derives its cultural imagery from neighbouring China and Korea but modern Tokyo takes its visual cue and scale from the West. What binds the city's sprawling collage of foreign influences is its ability to make everything appear specifically Japanese, uniquely Tokyo.

'TOKYO IS A HUNDRED TIMES MORE MODERN THAN PARIS.'

Henri Michaux, 1932

Destruction by earthquake in 1923 and U.S. firebombing in 1945 mean that even 'Old Tokyo' is new. The capital's 'ancient' sites are reconstructions, traditional in form but their 'historic' status now lost in a city of perpetual reinvention. There appears to be no urban planning outside 'new and now', trends pass quickly, rebuilding is continual. Tokyo is so modern it looks like the future. Bullet trains glide over Rainbow Bridge to Tokyo Big Sight, a convention centre constructed from inverted pyramids on an artificial island. Towering architectural facades are animated by 21st-century digital graphics. Giant images 'speak' through multiple sound systems to massed commuters in the streets below. The futuristic Los Angeles of the classic sci-fi movie *Blade Runner* was inspired by the intensely visual and ultra-modern metropolis of Tokyo.

Tokyo Big Sight, the international exhibition centre by Japanese architect Sato Sogo Keikaku (1994). Odaiba Island, Tokyo Bay.

Claes Oldenburg and Coosje van Bruggen's *Saw, Sawing* (1996), a statement on Japan's innovative industry and Tokyo's sense of the surreal. Odaiba Island, Tokyo Bay.

'TOKYO – FINALLY A COUNTRY WHERE PEOPLE REALLY UNDERSTAND THE IMPORTANCE OF BEING URBAN.'

Urban C. Lehner, *Asian Wall Street Journal*, 1990

Its sheer size, modernity and affluence invite indulgence but to Western eyes the semiotics can be confusing. Fashion stores display the logos of globalization yet Tokyo youth finds sartorial inspiration in theatre and fantasy. Doorways in the Shinjuku red-light district use childlike imagery from Japanese *manga* cartoons to advertise 'adults only' services. Akihabara's electronics stores spill on to the street like hi-tech market stalls. After dark, the flashing neon signs of Love Hotels and Pachinko game parlours promise forms of fun that are quintessentially Tokyo.

Donald Richie likened Tokyo to the Buddhist maxim *shogyo mujo* – 'All is transient, impermanent, all is in motion – life is illusory'. Street graphics embody *shogyo mujo*. This book records that ephemeral process in 2001.

Wind carries the prayers for children who have died, represented by 'Mizuko Jizo' figures in Zojo-Ji shrine, Shiba-koen district.

TRADITION

1

'ONE OF THE UNIQUE JAPANESE CHARACTERISTICS IS A COMMON CONSCIOUSNESS. WE WANT TO PRESERVE IT.'

Naoki Izumiya, Asahi Corporation, 1995

Shrine figures representing the Bodhisattva 'Jizo', Yanaka cemetery.

'Mizuko Jizo', miniature 'Jizo' child memorial figures, Zojo-Ji shrine.

Overleaf: A Kanji computer font replaces traditional brush calligraphy. Advertisement detail, Shibuya subway station.

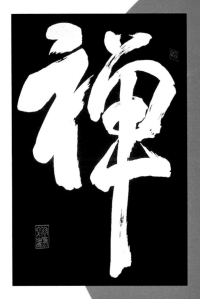

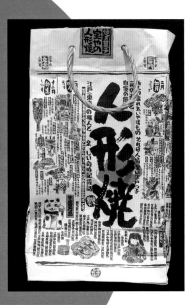

Kanji calligraphy (*shodo*) – prints on a souvenir 'Zen' T-shirt, a giant lantern at Senso-Ji temple
and a cake-store carrier bag. Opposite, traditional Hachimaki headbands on sale
in Asakusa are displayed in see-through pockets with English text on the front.
The 'Japan' headband has been put in its pocket upside down.

万 ● 歳

神 KAMI·KAZE 風

¥ JAPAN 日

BANZAI!!

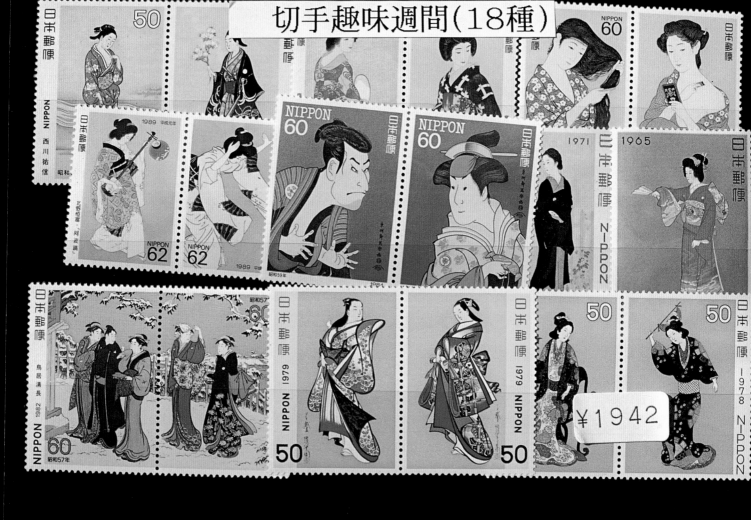

切手趣味週間（18種）

¥1942

Kimono designs on postage stamps and street performers.

Kimonos worn at weddings, festivals and depicted on flea-market ephemera.

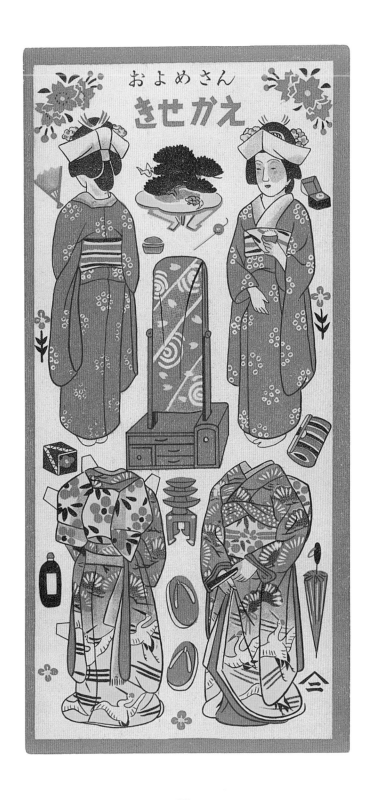

おまかせOK!

OK便

Keihin ケイヒン陸運

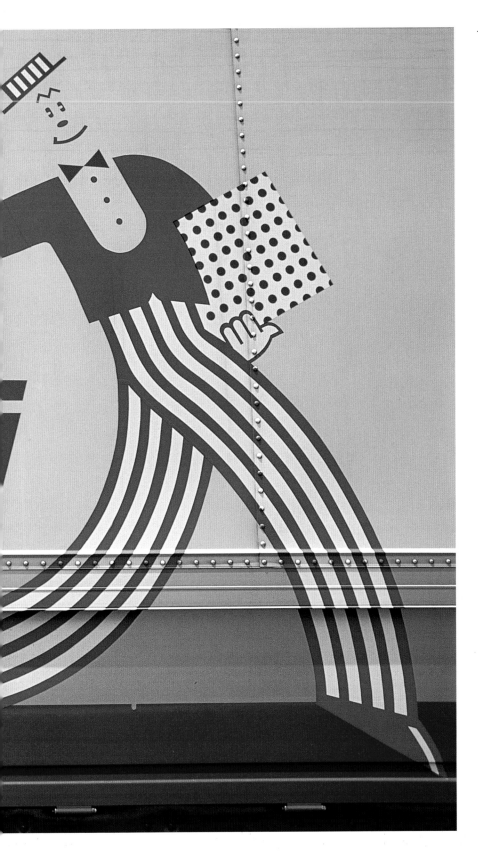

The logo livery of a courier-service vehicle.

SIGNS SYMBOLS AND SERVICES

2

宅急便

'TOKYO'S STREETS DO NOT SPEAK IN THE MEASURED ACCENTS OF EUROPE'S CAPITALS.'

Donald Richie, *Tokyo: a View of the City*, 1999

Speed and care are embodied in the cat logos of courier services.

Courier company logos signify fast and personal service.

Street signs denoting a footpath, a fire hydrant and a cycle way, and an automated traffic cop.

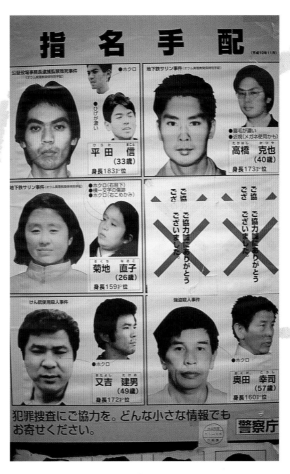

'Wanted' posters featuring suspected Aum Shinrikyo cult members.
The cartoon mouse character Pi-Po represents the Tokyo police force.

Overleaf: A waving cat, a popular symbol of good luck, adorns
patron's lockers in the streets of Shinjuku's red-light district.

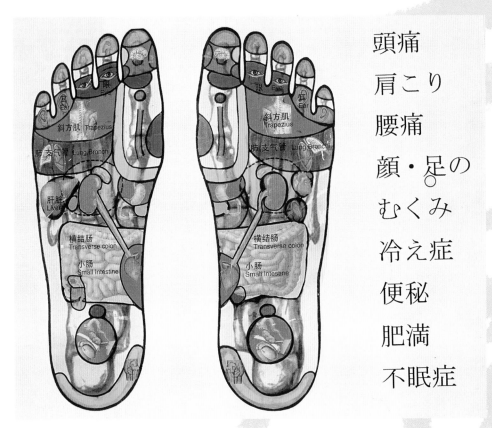

頭痛
肩こり
腰痛
顔・足の
むくみ
冷え症
便秘
肥満
不眠症

Signs for services – foot massage and clean water.

第42回水道週間懸賞募集特選　椎　文香さん（宮城南小学校5年生）

「水道は豊かな社会のいのちづな」

おいしい水

水道週間
6月1日（金）～7日（木）

The Niimi Building in Tokyo's wholesale restaurant district of Kappabashi.

FOOD AND DRINK 3

'THE USUAL WAY IN WHICH JAPANESE MEN PASS A DULL DAY IS IN FEASTING AND DRINKING.'

Rev. W. E. Griffis, 1873

Restaurant signs and plastic menu displays.

Overleaf: Cake store, Asakusa market.

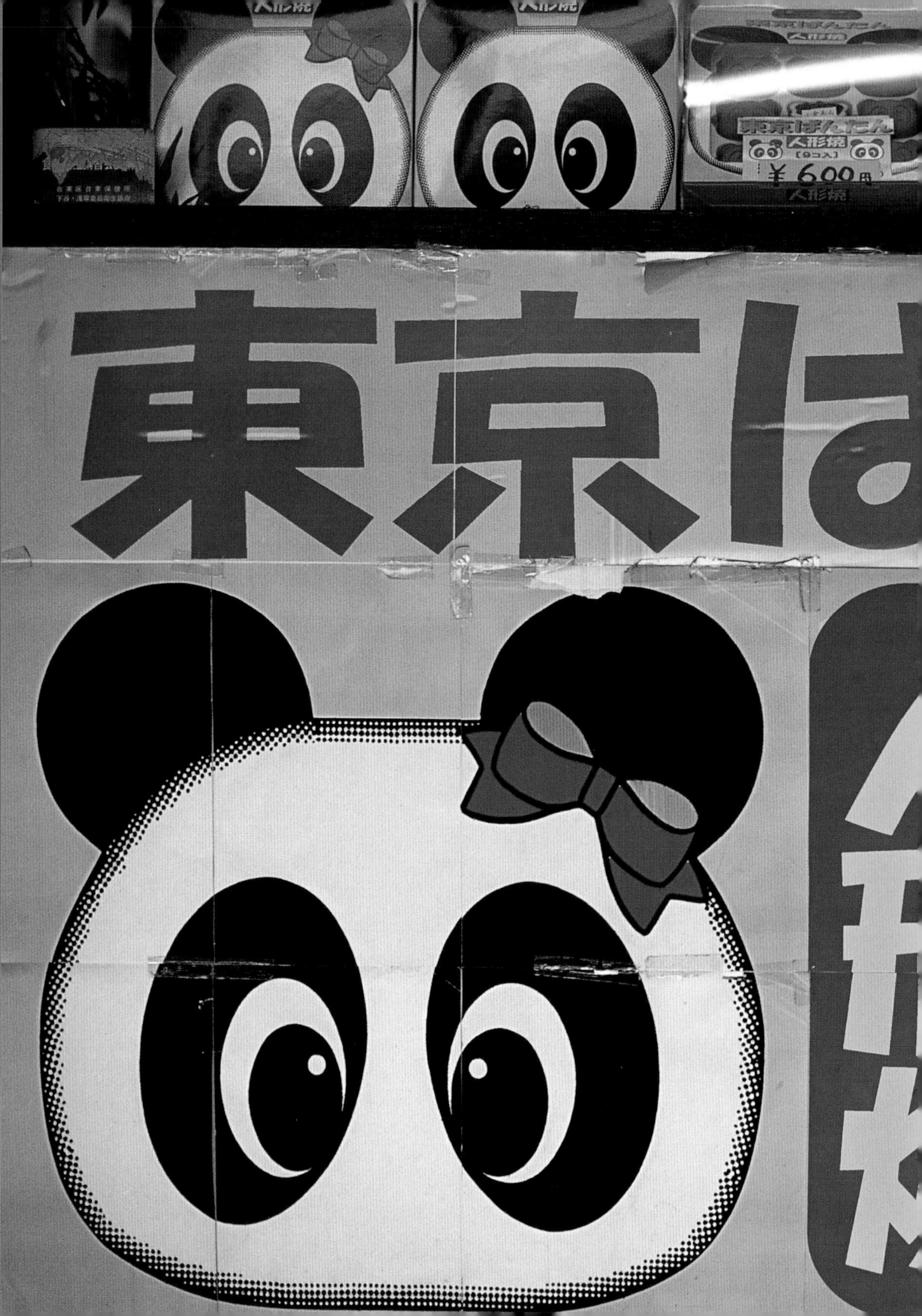
東京
人形焼
【9コ入】
¥600円

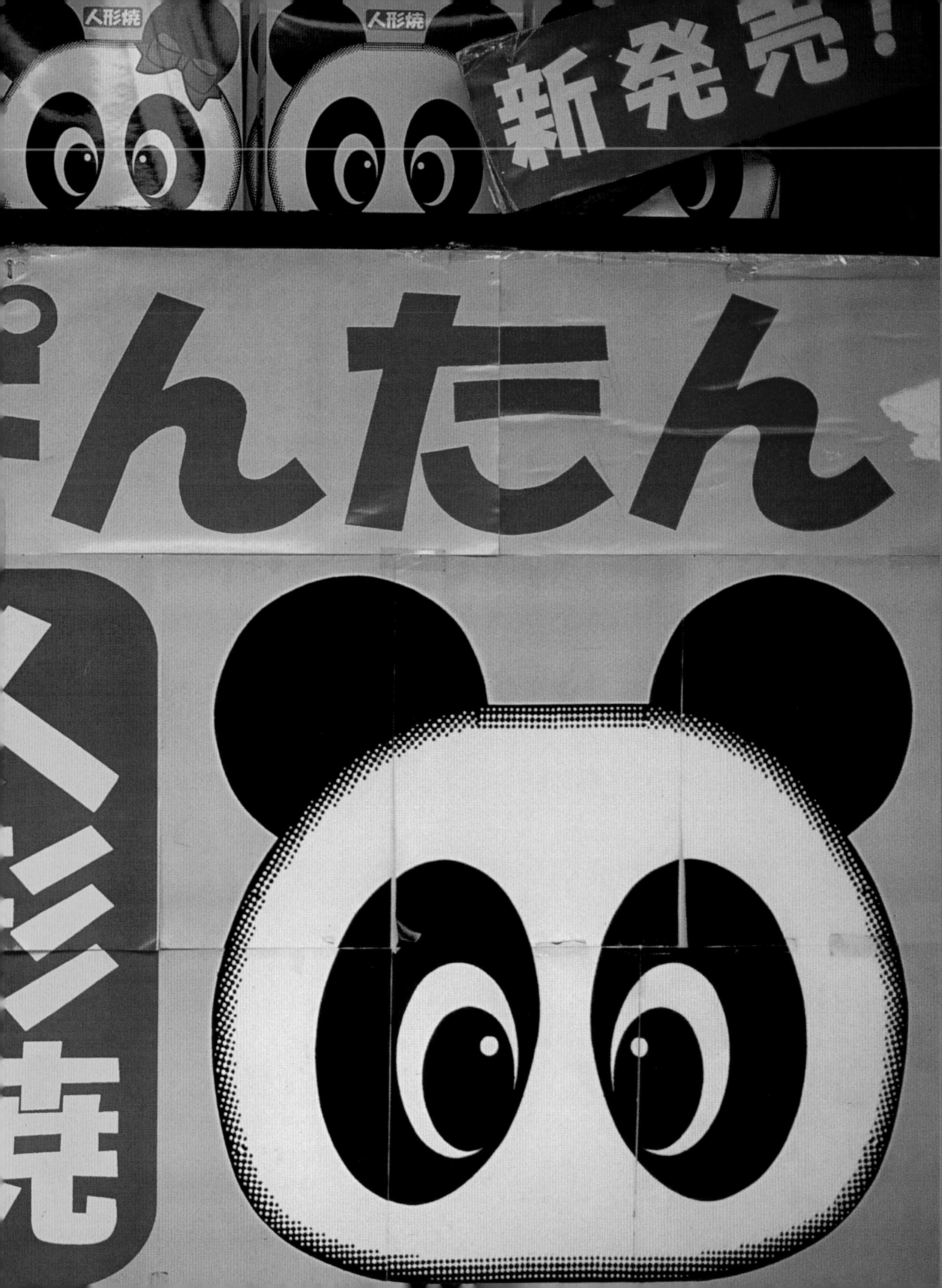
人形焼
人形焼
新発売!
んたん

Cake packaging, Asakusa market.

International and national brands in Tokyo's ubiquitous vending machines.

Window display of the Wako department store in Tokyo's affluent Ginza district.

FASHION

4

'CLOTHING WITHOUT PREJUDICE.'

Harajuku fashion store sign

Dressing up, meeting friends and photographing each other – Harajuku's Sunday catwalk, the JR railway bridge.

Overleaf: Elements of Kabuki theatre, Geisha and other traditional arts are freely associated with pop-culture themes.

Harajuku 'Goth' gatherings of the 1990s developed into
a weekly street theatre by Tokyo high-school youth.

Swastikas and black leather –
fashion not fascism.

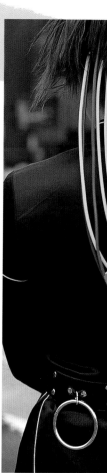

Science-fiction and bondage-inspired accessories – school's out.

A neon sign pulses to the beat of karaoke
in a Shinjuku night-club window.

MUSIC

5

'SINGING MAKES MY HEART FEEL GOOD.'

Mr Japanese Crazy Boy, karaoke singer, Tokyo, 1981

A karaoke bar sign in the Roppongi district and a T-shirt combining traditional imagery with rock and roll.

Rock & roll – emblazoned on the entrances to clubs and karaoke bars and enshrined in a museum.

Printed and sprayed stencil-style imagery promoting pop music.

Overleaf: A Pop-art style rendition of legendary stencil image
'Andre the Giant' by American artist Shepard Fairey.

が衝突した
方
さ
東
4
3
POSTAL PARCEL
CC445806565JP
CP72
JAPAN
FROM
TO

1950s styling on a flea-market original record, a revival band poster and a club entrance.

Sign over a club doorway in Shinjuku's Kabuki-cho street.

SEX 6

'THE JAPANESE ARE REALLY WITHOUT ANY SENSE OF SIN, AND HAVE NO WORD IN THEIR LANGUAGE TO EXPRESS THE IDEA EXACTLY.'

Rev. R. B. Perry, 1897

Manga cartoon imagery – street comic stall and sandwich-board details.

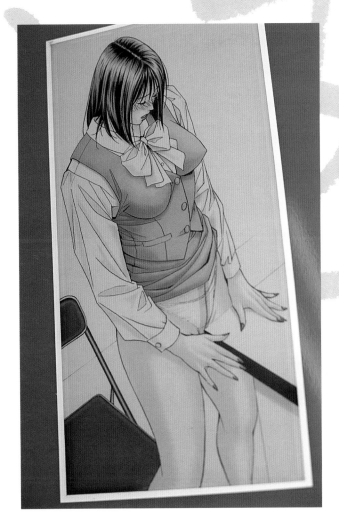

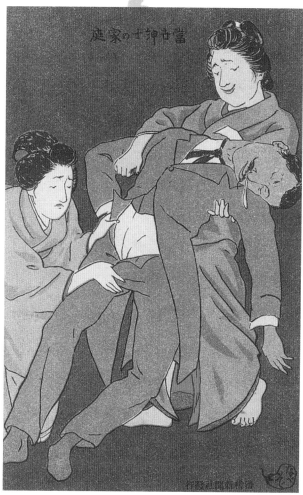

Erotic imagery on the sex-club doorways of modern Tokyo and early 20th-century postcards from flea markets.

Overleaf: *Manga* calling cards in the public phone booths of Shinjuku's red-light district.

S & M imagery on sex-club signs in Kabuki-Cho, Shinjuku's red-light district, and a flea-market postcard (1907).

MISTRESS

fetish bar

4f

OPEN 20:00 ~

MASTERS

bondage bar

3f

OPEN 20:00 ~

(03) - 3585 - 5133

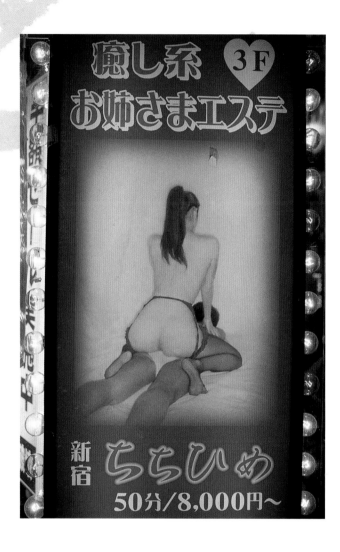

Illuminated signs and stairwell to Kabuki-Cho sex clubs.

A vending machine and advertisement
for self-assembly erotic *manga* dolls.
Akihabara district.

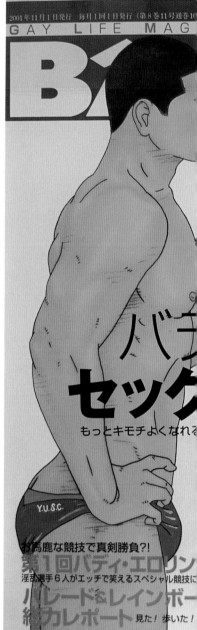

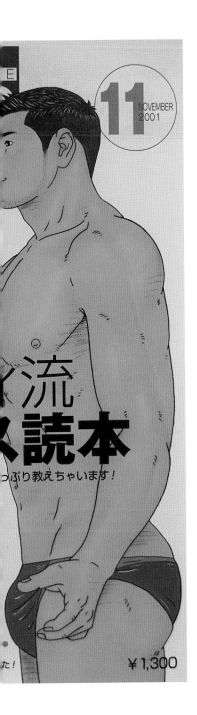

Magazine covers displayed outside the stores and clubs of Shinjuku's gay district.

Digital advertising imagery with wrap-around sound assails Tokyo's masses. Shibuya-Ku.

DIGITAL 7

'GOSH, YOU'VE REALLY GOT SOME NICE TOYS HERE.'

Roy Batty, Nexus 6 replicant, 2019 (from *Blade Runner*, 1982)

Robot pets in Akihabara's electronics market.

Popular robot figures in toy-store window displays, Asakusa.

Details from stalls and window displays in Akihabara's electronics market.

Shinjuku and Shibuya – districts of Tokyo that inspired the cityscapes of Ridley Scott's classic sci-fi film *Blade Runner*.

Detail from the shirt of an antique toy dealer, featuring 1950s tin robot toys.

NOSTALGIA

8

'IT IS SAID THAT WHAT IS CALLED "THE SPIRIT OF THE AGE" IS SOMETHING TO WHICH ONE CANNOT RETURN.'

Yamamoto Tsunetomo, Samurai, 1716

Flea-market ephemera – a 1950s pop-up street scene, a 1930s poster with Imperial imagery and a card collection featuring 1940s theatre stars.

Astro Boy, created in 1952 by the father of modern *manga*,
Tezuka Osamu, celebrates his 50th anniversary on
a breakfast cereal packet and a T-shirt.

1950s magazine covers in Tokyo's flea markets.

Traditional plastic dolls, masks and toys remain popular in hi-tech Tokyo.

Overleaf: Collectable phone cards in a Tokyo flea market.

'THE END IS IMPORTANT IN ALL THINGS.'

Yamamoto Tsunetomo, Samurai, 1716